HAL•LEONARD
INSTRUMENTAL PLAY-ALONG

AUDIO
ACCESS
INCLUDED

PLAYBACK+
eed • Pitch • Balance • Loop

FLUTE

Disney
CLASSICS

T0039768

To access audio visit:
www.halleonard.com/mylibrary

Enter Code
4535-1881-5157-5426

The following songs are the property of:
BOURNE CO.
Music Publishers • 5 West 37th Street • New York, NY 10018
Baby Mine, Give a Little Whistle, Heigh-Ho, I've Got No Strings, Some Day My Prince Will Come,
When You Wish Upon a Star, Whistle While You Work, Who's Afraid of the Big Bad Wolf?

Disney characters and artwork © Disney Enterprises, Inc.

ISBN 978-1-4584-1596-7

WALT DISNEY MUSIC COMPANY
WONDERLAND MUSIC COMPANY, INC.

DISTRIBUTED BY

HAL•LEONARD®
7777 W. BLUEMOUND RD. P.O. BOX 13819 MILWAUKEE, WI 53213

Disney characters and artwork © Disney Enterprises, Inc.

Visit Hal Leonard Online at
www.halleonard.com

ALICE IN WONDERLAND

from Walt Disney's ALICE IN WONDERLAND

Flute

Words by BOB HILLIARD
Music by SAMMY FAIN

BABY MINE
from Walt Disney's DUMBO

FLUTE

Words by NED WASHINGTON
Music by FRANK CHURCHILL

BELLA NOTTE

(This Is the Night)

from Walt Disney's LADY AND THE TRAMP

Flute

Words and Music by PEGGY LEE
and SONNY BURKE

GIVE A LITTLE WHISTLE

from Walt Disney's PINOCCHIO

FLUTE

Words by NED WASHINGTON
Music by LEIGH HARLINE

HEIGH-HO

The Dwarfs' Marching Song from Walt Disney's SNOW WHITE AND THE SEVEN DWARFS

Flute

Words by LARRY MOREY
Music by FRANK CHURCHILL

I'VE GOT NO STRINGS

from Walt Disney's PINOCCHIO

Flute

Words by NED WASHINGTON
Music by LEIGH HARLINE

LITTLE APRIL SHOWER

from Walt Disney's BAMBI

Flute

Words by LARRY MOREY
Music by FRANK CHURCHILL

ONCE UPON A DREAM

from Walt Disney's SLEEPING BEAUTY

Flute

Words and Music by SAMMY FAIN
and JACK LAWRENCE
Adapted from a Theme by Tchaikovsky

SOME DAY MY PRINCE WILL COME

from Walt Disney's SNOW WHITE AND THE SEVEN DWARFS

Words by LARRY MOREY
Music by FRANK CHURCHILL

FLUTE

THE UNBIRTHDAY SONG

from Walt Disney's ALICE IN WONDERLAND

Flute

Words and Music by MACK DAVID,
AL HOFFMAN and JERRY LIVINGSTON

WHEN YOU WISH UPON A STAR

from Walt Disney's PINOCCHIO

FLUTE

Words by NED WASHINGTON
Music by LEIGH HARLINE

Slowly, with feeling

WHISTLE WHILE YOU WORK

from Walt Disney's SNOW WHITE AND THE SEVEN DWARFS

Flute

Words by LARRY MOREY
Music by FRANK CHURCHILL

WHO'S AFRAID OF THE BIG BAD WOLF?

from Walt Disney's THREE LITTLE PIGS

FLUTE

Words and Music by FRANK CHURCHILL
Additional Lyric by ANN RONELL

YOU CAN FLY! YOU CAN FLY! YOU CAN FLY!

from Walt Disney's PETER PAN

Words by SAMMY CAHN
Music by SAMMY FAIN

FLUTE